THE SABBATH

Activity Book

The Sabbath Activity Book

Bible Pathway Adventures® is a trademark of BPA Publishing Ltd.
Defenders of the Faith® is a trademark of BPA Publishing Ltd.

ISBN: 978-1-989961-43-8

Author: Pip Reid

Creative Director: Curtis Reid

For free Bible resources including coloring pages, worksheets, puzzles and more, visit our website at:

shop.biblepathwayadventures.com

◇ INTRODUCTION ◇

Children will love learning about the Sabbath with *The Sabbath Activity Book*. Packed with fun activities, worksheets, coloring pages and puzzles to help educators just like you teach children the Biblical faith. Includes detailed scripture references for easy Bible verse look-up, and a handy answer key for parents and teachers.

Bible Pathway Adventures helps educators teach children the Biblical faith in a fun and creative way. We do this via our Activity Books and free printable activities – available on our website: www.biblepathwayadventures.com

Thanks for buying this Activity Book and supporting our ministry. Every book purchased helps us continue our work providing free Classroom Packs and discipleship resources to families and missions around the world.

The search for Truth is more fun than Tradition!

◇◇ TABLE OF CONTENTS ◇◇

Creative writing

Crafts & Projects

© BPA Publishing Ltd 2023

This book belongs to:

....

Draw something

On the Sabbath I...

The Sabbath

The Sabbath is first mentioned in Genesis where the seventh day was set apart by God as a day of rest. Yeshua kept the Sabbath, and as His disciples we need to follow His example. For believers in Messiah, the Sabbath is a wonderful blessing: a time for rest and fellowship. It begins at sunset on Friday and ends at sundown on Saturday. Did you know that remembering the Sabbath is one of the ten commandments, and is mentioned throughout the Torah?

"Remember the Sabbath and keep it Holy. You shall work six days, and do all your work, but the seventh day is a Sabbath to God. You shall not do any work in it, you, nor your son, nor your daughter, your male servant, nor your female servant, nor your livestock, nor your stranger who is within your gates." (Exodus 20:8-10)

Honoring the Sabbath is still relevant for us today. Yeshua said: "Don't think that I came to destroy the Torah or the prophets. I didn't come to destroy, but to fulfill. For most certainly, I tell you, until heaven and earth pass away, not even one smallest letter or one tiny pen stroke shall in any way pass away from the Torah, until all things are accomplished." (Matthew 5:17-18)

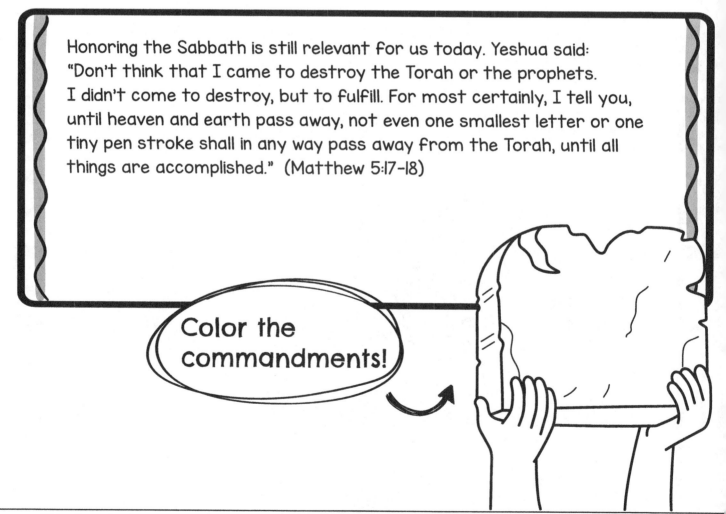

Color the commandments!

"Remember the Sabbath. Keep it Holy."

(Exodus 20:8)

What's the Word?

Read Genesis 2:1-7 (ESV). Using the words below,
fill in the blanks to complete the Bible passage.

HEAVENS	RESTED	CREATION	FORMED
FINISHED	BLESSED	EARTH	BREATH
SEVENTH	HOLY	MIST	LIVING

" Thus the .... and the earth were ...., and all the host of them. And on the .... day God finished His work that He had done, and He .... on the seventh day from all His work that he had done. So God .... the seventh day and made it ...., because on it God rested from all His work that He had done in .... These are the generations of the heavens and the earth when they were created, in the day that God made the .... and the heavens. When no bush of the field was yet in the land and no small plant of the field had yet sprung up - for God had not caused it to rain on the land, and there was no man to work the ground, and a ....

as going up from the land and was watering the whole face of the ground - then God .... the man of dust from the ground and breathed into his nostrils the .... of life, and the man became a .... creature. "

The CREATION

Read Genesis 1-2. Find and circle the words below.

```
Y  S  Y  P  T  D  M  G  B  X  P  K  I  Y  T
T  E  H  Y  N  U  G  S  L  M  C  K  I  C  N
C  A  V  U  P  C  Z  C  E  V  F  T  X  O  I
F  S  H  G  M  E  T  M  S  E  W  E  A  M  G
S  S  I  H  U  A  Q  H  S  V  D  A  L  H  H
T  E  A  A  J  R  M  Y  E  F  G  S  E  E  T
G  K  V  B  P  T  Q  K  D  O  G  E  F  A  M
V  Y  J  E  B  H  V  W  A  S  V  A  E  V  E
I  Q  P  Y  N  A  E  R  S  M  O  S  C  E  B
X  K  S  F  F  D  T  L  R  H  X  O  B  N  S
R  X  U  F  H  C  A  H  N  Q  M  N  U  S  H
R  E  C  U  D  G  D  Y  B  T  V  S  G  D  G
T  U  S  P  U  I  K  P  S  H  H  C  F  T  X
U  H  G  T  E  W  R  S  P  I  R  I  T  I  N
T  A  H  E  L  O  H  I  M  E  R  D  A  Y  M
```

SEAS

SPIRIT

EARTH

BLESSED

NIGHT

DAY

SABBATH

SEASONS

ELOHIM

HEAVENS

REST

SEVEN DAYS

Sabbath in the wilderness

Moses said to the Israelites, "This is what God has spoken, 'Tomorrow is a solemn rest, a holy Sabbath to Yahweh. Bake that which you want to bake and boil that which you want to boil, and store the rest until the morning.'" They stored the manna until the morning as Moses asked, and it did not become foul and there were no worms in it. Moses said, "Eat that today, for today is a Sabbath to God. Today you shall not find manna in the field. Six days you shall gather it, but on the seventh day is the Sabbath. There shall be no manna." On the seventh day, some of the people went out to gather manna and they found none. God said to Moses, "How long do you refuse to keep My commandments and My laws? Behold, because God has given you the Sabbath, therefore he gives you on the sixth day the bread of two days. Everyone stay in his place. Let no one go out of his place on the seventh day." So the people rested on the seventh day. (Exodus 16:23-30)

How did the Israelites find food in the wilderness?

....

Why could the Israelites not find manna on the Sabbath?

....

....

....

....

....

"The people of Israel shall keep the Sabbath, observing the Sabbath throughout their generations..."

(Exodus 31:16)

Twelve tribes of Israel

After the Israelites left Egypt, they spent 40 years in the wilderness learning the Torah before they reached the land of Canaan. The Israelites were split into twelve tribes, although in fact there were thirteen tribes. Each tribe was named after a son or grandson of Israel (Jacob); eleven of Jacob's sons headed one tribe each, while the descendants of Joseph became two separate tribes (Ephraim and Manasseh). Why do you think God divided the Israelites into tribes? Where are the tribes today? Color the banners from the twelve tribes of Israel mentioned in Numbers 1:1-15 and 13:4-15.

ISSACHAR

JUDAH

ZEBULUN

NAPHTALI

ASHER

DAN

Twelve tribes of Israel

GAD

SIMEON

REUBEN

EPHRAIM

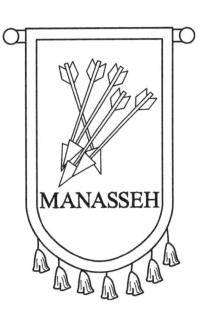

MANASSEH

BENJAMIN

Manna in the wilderness

Help the Israelites gather manna (except on the Sabbath!)

Wilderness of Paran

The
Sinai Times

LAND OF MIDIAN   A Bible History publication

Sabbath rules

....

....

....

....

....

....

No manna on Sabbath

....

....

....

....

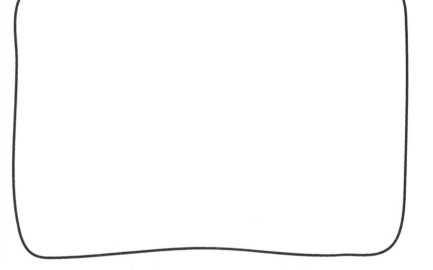

Quail in camp!

"At twilight you shall eat meat, and in the morning you shall be filled with bread."

(Exodus 16:12)

Sabbath instructions

How should we honor the Sabbath? The Bible tells us to set apart the seventh day of each week as a holy day, to rest from our work, not pursue our own interests, assemble with other believers, give an offering, and not buy or sell, or conduct commerce. Why is it important to honor the Sabbath today? What do you do on the Sabbath?

Read Exodus 16-20, Leviticus 23, Numbers 28, Nehemiah 10 – 13, Isaiah 58, and Jeremiah 17. Write six Bible references that describe the Sabbath. Color the Israelite.

....

....

....

....

....

....

Keeping the Sabbath

"Remember that you were a slave in the land of Egypt, and God brought you out from there with a mighty hand and an outstretched arm. Therefore, He commanded you to keep the Sabbath day." (Deuteronomy 5:15)

Read Exodus I. Answer the questions.

Who did the new king of Egypt not know?

....

What did the Egyptians do to oppress the people of Israel?

....

....

What did the Israelites build for Pharaoh?

....

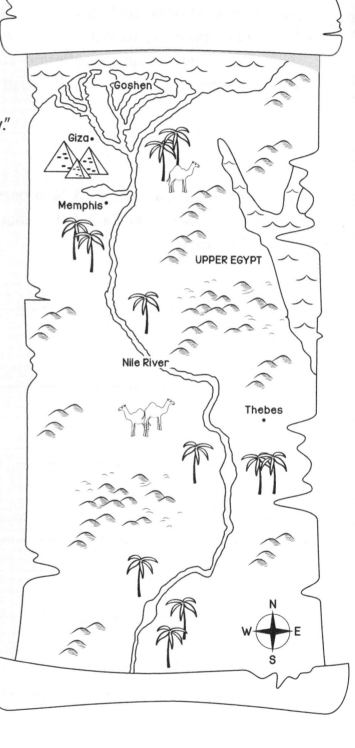

Discovering tzitzits

Tzitzits, also known as tassels, are a traditional Israelite garment used to fulfill one of God's commandments. In Numbers 15:37-41, God instructed the Israelites to attach fringes to the four corners of their garments to remind them of His commandments and to serve as a visual representation of the faith.

"Speak to the people of Israel, and tell them to make tassels on the corners of their garments throughout their generations, and to put a cord of blue on the tassel of each corner. It shall be a tassel for you to look at and remember all the commandments of Yahweh, to do them, not to follow after your own heart and your own eyes, which you are inclined to whore after.
So, you shall remember and do all My commandments, and be holy to your God.
I am the Yahweh, who brought you out of the land of Egypt…"

For thousands of years, tzitzits have been a part of Israelite culture. They are usually made of wool or linen, and are white and blue. The Bible includes instructions on how to make tzitzits; they should have four strands of wool or linen, each strand knotted twice. The strands should be twisted together seven times, and a blue thread should be added to the strands. The blue thread is known as a tekhelet and is a very important part of the tzitzits. It is a reminder of God's covenant with the Israelites. Tzitzits are worn around the waist of the wearer and are a reminder of the commandments of God. They are a symbol of religious faith and are worn by Israelites around the world who desire to honor God's commandments.

Read Numbers 15 and the article above.
Answer the questions below.

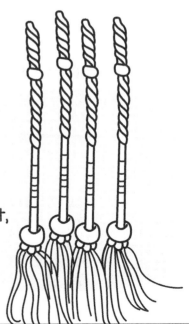

1. What are tzitzits?

2. What material are tzitzits usually made of?

3. What is the significance of the blue thread, or tekhelet, that is added to the strands of tzitzits?

The ten commandments

Read Exodus 20:1-17. Fill in the blanks with the words at the bottom of the page.

1. I am .... your God. You will have no other gods before Me.

2. You shall make no ....

3. You shall not take the .... of God in vain.

4. Remember the .... and keep it holy.

5. Honor your .... and mother.

6. Do not ....

7. Do not commit ....

8. Do not ....

9. Do not give .... testimony against your neighbor.

10. Do not .... other people's things.

SABBATH   COVET
FATHER   ADULTERY
STEAL   YAHWEH
MURDER   IDOLS
FALSE   NAME

The ten commandments

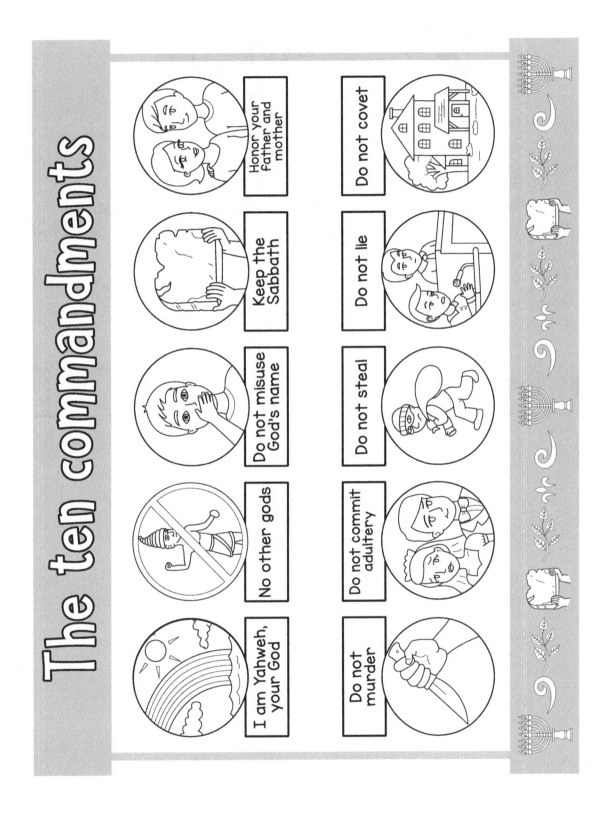

seven

On the 7th day, God finished His work that He had done and rested.
He blessed the 7th day and made it holy. Trace the number 7.

(tracing row of dashed number 7s)

Write multiples of seven in the boxes below.

7	14						

How many fingers are there?

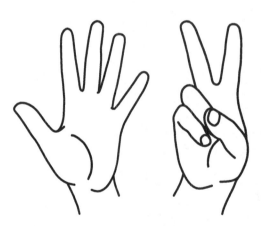 

I honor the Sabbath by…

....

Sabbath song

(Isaiah 58:13-14)

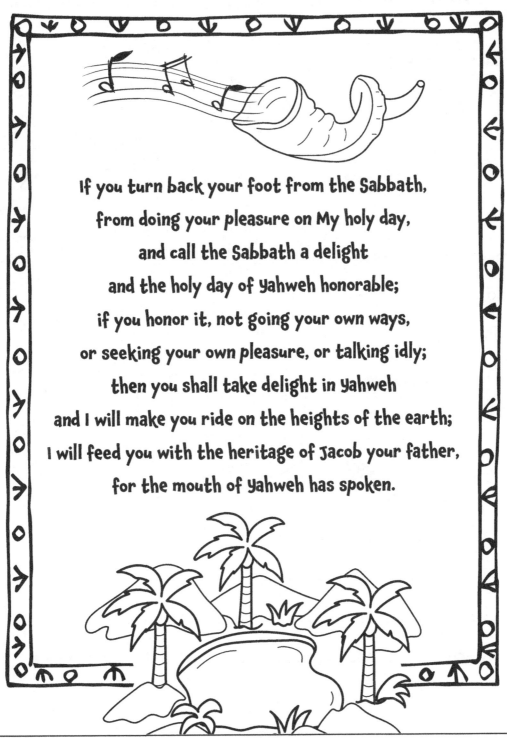

If you turn back your foot from the Sabbath,

from doing your pleasure on My holy day,

and call the Sabbath a delight

and the holy day of Yahweh honorable;

if you honor it, not going your own ways,

or seeking your own pleasure, or talking idly;

then you shall take delight in Yahweh

and I will make you ride on the heights of the earth;

I will feed you with the heritage of Jacob your father,

for the mouth of Yahweh has spoken.

Ark of the Covenant

The ten commandments were placed in the ark of the covenant (Hebrews 9:4). Read Exodus 25:1-22. This Bible passage describes the measurements for the ark and mercy seat. Fill in the blank spaces below. Color the ark.

Measurements for the mercy seat:

.... long

.... wide

Measurements for the ark:

.... long

.... wide

.... high

The ark and poles were made of ....

The ark and poles were overlaid with ....

The rings, lid of atonement and cherubim were made of ....

There were .... cherubim, ... rings, and .... poles.

Moses reminded the Israelites to honor the Sabbath.
Read Deuteronomy 5:12-15 (ESV).
Unscramble the words to learn this commandment.

vrebseo	....	dmcdomnae	....
bhaSabt	....	oonserrju	....
vtsehen	....	hmityg nhda	....
sret	....	erntsva	....
tygEp	....	yloh	....

✳ Read Moses' speech to the Israelites in Deuteronomy 5:1-33.

A Hebrew day

The seventh day is the biblical Sabbath. When God finished creating the earth, He rested on the seventh day. He blessed this day and made it holy, or 'set-apart' (Genesis 2:1-3). Because we use the Gregorian calendar, people usually think of days beginning and ending at midnight. But on the Hebrew calendar, a day starts and ends at nightfall. The Sabbath begins at sunset on Friday and lasts until sundown on Saturday.

A Hebrew day starts at nightfall (approx 6pm)

Day and night on the Gregorian calendar is from midnight to midnight

The Sabbath

Write a list of things you do every Sabbath.

Imagine you are a Hebrew living in Capernaum at the time of Yeshua. What would you have done on the Sabbath?

Where in the Bible can I find the commandment to honor the Sabbath?

Draw a picture of Paul teaching on the Sabbath in Pisidian Antioch (Acts 13).

The Appointed Times

Are there days other than the weekly Sabbath that are observed as a Sabbath? Yes! Both the Spring and Fall Feasts include Sabbath days. The Feast of Unleavened Bread (Hag Ha-Matzot) immediately follows the Passover meal and lasts for seven days. The first and seventh days of this feast are Sabbaths. On these days, no customary work can be done. The Feast of Pentecost (Shavu'ot) takes place 50 days after the day of First Fruits (Yom KaBikkurim), where Yeshua was offered up as the Firstfruit of all who died (1 Corinthians 15:20). Pentecost commemorates a time of thanksgiving for the grain harvest. On this day, the holy spirit (Ru'ach HaKodesh) was given at the temple in Jerusalem (Acts 2). Pentecost is a Sabbath day, and no customary work can be done.

During the Fall Feasts, the day of Trumpets (Yom Teru'ah) occurs on the first day of the seventh month, and is a Sabbath. However, it does not fall on the seventh day of the week. On this day, no customary work can be done. The day of Atonement (Yom Kippur) occurs once a year, on the 10th day of the seventh month, and is a Sabbath. However, it does not fall on the seventh day of the week. On this day, no customary work can be done. The Feast of Tabernacles (Sukkot) lasts for seven days. The first day of this Feast is a Sabbath. The eighth day (known as The Last Great Day, or Shemini Atzeret) is a Sabbath. On these days, no customary work can be done.

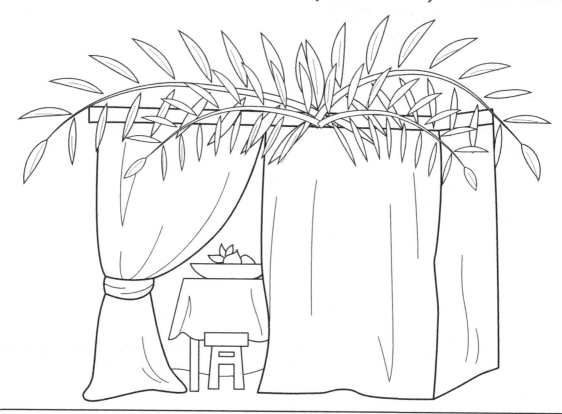

The Appointed Times

What is the difference between a Sabbath and a high Sabbath? A high Sabbath is an annual holy day, or annual Sabbath, as commanded in Leviticus 23. A high Sabbath occurs when one of the holy days coincides with the weekly Sabbath. This weekly Sabbath is a day to keep holy (set-apart), but these annual holy days take precedence if they occur on the seventh-day Sabbath.

1. How did Yeshua fulfil the Spring Feasts?

2. How many high Sabbaths will occur this year?

   ....

3. How do you honor Sukkot?

   ....

Sabbath word match

Which books of the Bible mention the Sabbath?
Match the books below with the correct statement.

1 Paul taught in the synagogue on the Sabbath in Pisidian Antioch.

....

2 God rested on the seventh day and made it holy.

....

3 Mary, Mary Magdalene and Salome waited until after the Sabbath to buy spices.

....

4 Paul went to the synagogue every Sabbath while he stayed in Corinth.

....

5 Remember the Sabbath day and keep it Holy.

....

6 So there remains a Sabbath rest for God's people.

....

7 How blessed is a man who keeps from profaning the Sabbath.

....

8 Observe My Sabbath and keep it Holy.

....

9 "The Sabbath was made for man, not man for the Sabbath."

....

10 When He came to Nazareth, Yeshua went to the synagogue on the Sabbath day.

....

A. Acts 18
B. Exodus 20
C. Acts 13
D. Hebrews 4
E. Genesis 2

F. Exodus 31
G. Mark 16
H. Isaiah 56
I. Luke 4
J. Mark 2

The SABBATH

**Read Deuteronomy 5, 20, Mark 2 and Acts 13-18.
Answer the questions below.**

1. On which day did Paul enter the synagogue in Acts 13:14?

2. Who gathered to hear Paul teach on the Sabbath in Acts 13:44?

3. Where did Paul meet with a group on the Sabbath in Acts 16?

4. On how many Sabbaths did Paul discuss the Scriptures in the synagogue?

5. In which city did Paul do this?

6. What had been taught in synagogues every Sabbath since ancient times?

7. When Paul reached Corinth, what did he do every Sabbath?

8. Who did Yeshua say the Sabbath was made for?

9. What day did God tell His people to keep holy?

10. What does God tell His people to do on the Sabbath?

The Sabbath

Open your Bible and read Hebrews 4:9-11.

Copy the scriptures on the lines provided.
Color the illustration at the bottom of the page.

....

....

....

....

....

....

....

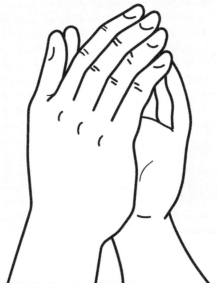

The Sabbath

Read Mark 3:1-6. Write a summary of this Bible passage below.

....

....

....

1. What does God tell us to do on the Sabbath? (Deuteronomy 5)

....

....

2. Which day did God tell His people to keep holy? (Exodus 20)

....

....

3. How many days can God's people work each week? (Leviticus 23)

....

....

Draw your favorite scene from this story.

What could the Sabbath teach me?	On the Sabbath I...
....	....
....	....

A 1st century synagogue

In Bible times, Israelites often met in synagogues on the Sabbath. Because the Greek word 'synagōgē' means an assembly, gathering, or even a congregation, the oldest form of synagogue was a market square or city gate. Only a few towns in Judea were wealthy enough to have a building dedicated to learning and prayer. Instead, people mostly assembled in the house of the village chief, a market square, or a courtyard to discuss important issues.

By the 1st century, some synagogues in Judea had become a type of community center where Israelites regularly gathered for events, discussions, legal proceedings, and to read the Torah on the Sabbath. For people scattered throughout the Roman Empire, synagogues gave them a sense of community and knowledge. In New Testament times, Yeshua entered synagogues in the Galilee to discuss the scriptures. When the apostle Paul journeyed through Asia Minor, he frequently joined Sabbath gatherings both in outdoor and indoor settings (Acts 16:13).

Color the synagogue!

A 1ˢᵗ century synagogue

What did the inside of a synagogue look like? Recently, the ruins of synagogues dating back to the 1ˢᵗ century were uncovered by archaeologists in the land of Israel. They found the buildings shared certain characteristics. They were built from stone with a stone foundation, and were square-shaped, sometimes with a simple inscription stating that it was a house of prayer. Inside, there were very few decorations. People sat on stairs or benches around the walls, and faced the center of the room where readings and teaching took place from a lectern and chair. There was an 'ark' box or niche that held valuable Torah scrolls. Rooms were large so roofs were supported by stone columns. Synagogue buildings often had baths (miqveh) for ritual cleansing attached to them. Research 1ˢᵗ century synagogues and draw the inside of a synagogue at the time of Yeshua.

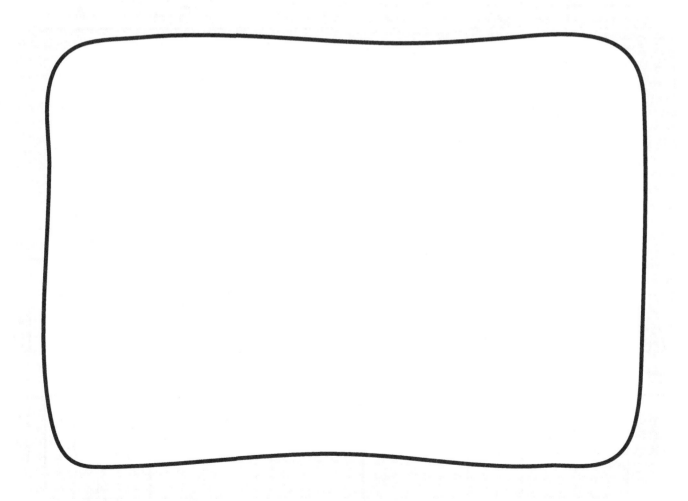

Did Yeshua keep the Sabbath?

Did Yeshua keep the Sabbath? Let's find out! The Bible verse below is written in code.
Use the chart at the bottom of the page to fill in the missing letters and crack the code!
Hint: Read Luke 4:16 (ESV)

A S _ A S _ _ S _ U S _ _ _ _ , _ _ _ _ _ _ _
14 9 6 14 9 24 2 9 22 1 9 4 13 7   24 3 6 3 16 4 4 13

_ _ _ S _ A _ _ U _ _ _ _ _ S A _ _ A _ _
4 24 3 9 26 16 14 5 13 5 1 3 13 16 4 24 3 9 14 17 17 14 4 24

_ A _ , A _ _ _ _ S _ _ _ _ U _ _ _ _ _ A _
21 14 26 14 16 21 24 3 9 14 13 13 21 1 20 4 13 23 3 14 21

A	B	C	D	E	F	G	H	I	J	K	L	M
14												4

N	O	P	Q	R	S	T	U	V	W	X	Y	Z
					9		1					

Honor the Sabbath

"Remember the Sabbath day, to keep it holy. You shall labor six days, and do all your work, but the seventh day is a Sabbath to Yahweh your God. You shall not do any work in it, you, nor your son, nor your daughter, your male servant, nor your female servant, nor your livestock, nor your stranger who is within your gates; for in six days Yahweh made heaven and earth, the sea, and all that is in them, and rested the seventh day; therefore Yahweh blessed the Sabbath day and made it holy." (Exodus 20:8-11)

How many words can you create from:

Honor the Sabbath

....

....

....

....

....

....

ASHER   JUDAH   SIMEON

The SABBATH

Read Genesis 2, Exodus 31, Deuteronomy 5, Leviticus 23 - 24,
Isaiah 58, Psalm118, Jeremiah 17, and 2 Chronicles 2.
Find and circle each of the words from the list below.

```
P Y B L E S S E D U H A C X W
P D E T R F U P S N F S O W I
S V E K T B J Q A S X C M T T
N E T L V R Y M B E Q B M R O
B O T L I Q D Q B V W T A G R
T W E A D G I N A E J V N X A
H Q K K P F H V T N M W D S H
K O B I H A C T H T D Z M J R
T Q L Y U X R E S H Q T E Z E
K O X Y M M P T Q D N J N E J
Q I H L W N V I B A B B T Q O
Z V F K Q C K W K Y T J K G I
A P P O I N T E D T I M E T C
E V E R L A S T I N G R X R E
V B M Q E Y E S H U A Y C P R
```

HOLY

DELIGHT

SET APART

BLESSED

EVERLASTING

REJOICE

TORAH

SEVENTH DAY

COMMANDMENT

SABBATH

YESHUA

APPOINTED TIME

Did you know?

The apostle Paul kept the Sabbath. When he appeared before Festus in Caesarea, he declared, "Neither against the law of the Jews, nor against the temple, nor against Caesar have I committed any offense." (Acts 25:8.) How could this be true if he had not kept the Sabbath? In all their accusations against Paul, the religious leaders never accused him of disregarding the Sabbath.

Read Acts 13:13-45. Draw Paul teaching on the Sabbath in Antioch of Pisidia.

The Pharisees

One Sabbath, Yeshua was going through the grain fields. His disciples began to pluck heads of grain. The Pharisees said to Him, "Why are they doing what is not lawful on the Sabbath?" He replied, "Have you never read what David did when he was in need and was hungry… how he entered the house of God… and ate the bread of the Presence, which it is not lawful for any but the priests to eat. He also gave it to those who were with him? The Sabbath was made for man, not man for the Sabbath." (Mark 2:23-28)

Who were the Pharisees? The Pharisees believed in the Torah, the prophets, and other writings. They were afraid that breaking the rules of the Torah would bring judgment on the Israelites, so they added extra written and oral laws to ensure everyone kept the law. The Pharisees placed more importance on obeying these written and oral laws than the instructions given to Moses (Matthew 23). They became unnecessarily strict about Sabbath observance, and had many rules on how to keep the Sabbath. They would have carefully scrutinized Yeshua's behavior and teachings.

1. Read John 3, Acts 5, and 26. Name three famous Pharisees.

2. Read Matthew 12:1-13. After Yeshua spoke to the Pharisees on the Sabbath, what did He do?

3. Name Yeshua's twelve disciples.

Amazing Pharisee facts

At the time of Yeshua, the Pharisees were part of the Sanhedrin, the Jewish Council. There were about 6,000 Pharisees in the land of Israel.

The word "Pharisee" is derived from the Ancient Greek word meaning 'set apart'.

Gamaliel was a Pharisee leader considered sympathetic to followers of the Way (Acts 5:17-42).

The Pharisees were the authorized interpreters of Jewish law. They held an illegal trial at night to condemn Yeshua (Matthew 26:57-67).

The Pharisees knew the letter of the Torah but not the spirit of the Torah. They often manipulated the law to suit their needs, and burdened others to adhere to the law in order to benefit themselves.

Sabbath song

(Psalm 92:12-15)

The righteous shall flourish like the palm tree.

He will grow like a cedar in Lebanon.

They are planted in Yahweh's house.

They will flourish in our God's courts.

They will still produce fruit in old age.

They will be full of sap and green,

to show that Yahweh is upright.

He is my rock and there is no

unrighteousness in Him.

"For the Son of Man is Master even of the Sabbath."

(Matthew 12:8)

Yeshua

The Hebrew name of the Messiah is Yeshua. Yeshua means, 'God is salvation'. Yeshua never brok
the Sabbath, although the religious leaders accused him of doing so. He said, "Do not think
that I have come to abolish the Law or the Prophets; I have not come to abolish them
but to fulfill them. I say to you, until heaven and earth pass away, not an iota,
not a dot, will pass from the Law until all is accomplished." (Matthew 5:17-18).

Yeshua

יֵשׁוּעַ

Trace His Hebrew name here:	Write His Hebrew name here:
יֵשׁוּעַ	

Let's write!

Practice writing the name 'Yeshua' on the lines below.

יֵשׁוּעַ

יֵשׁוּעַ

Try this on your own.
Remember that Hebrew is read from RIGHT to LEFT.

My Sabbath day activities

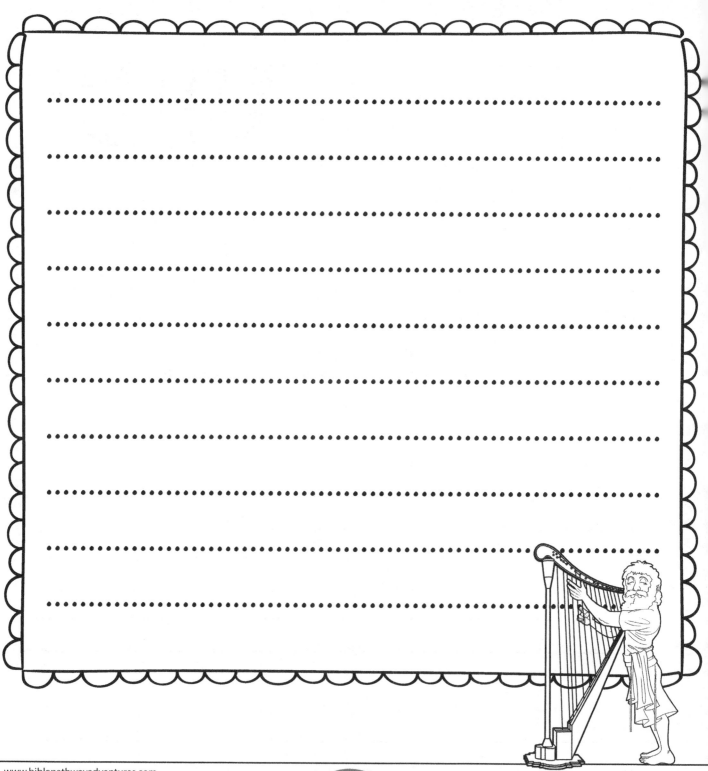

My Sabbath diary

Name: ....

Address: ....

During the Sabbath, I: ....

....

....

Color the menorah!

Draw a Sabbath activity.

The Sabbath

What did you do on the Sabbath?
Write an account of your day on the lines below.

....

....

....

....

....

....

....

....

....

....

....

....

Temple in Jerusalem

At the time of Yeshua, the temple in Jerusalem was the center of Israelite life. Israelites gathered at the temple on the weekly Sabbath to worship and learn together. They only had access to the temple courtyards and not the inside of the temple structure, but it was still considered a public building. The temple was run by a priestly aristocracy called the Sadducees. They were of the tribe of Levi and were responsible for overseeing the temple and offering sacrifices. On the Sabbath, they performed sacrificial offerings and prayers twice a day, with additional rites on High Sabbaths and Feast days. During the time of Roman rule, the temple was also the meeting place of the Sanhedrin, the highest court of Jewish law.

Did you know one of the reasons King Herod enlarged the Temple Mount was to accommodate huge numbers of pilgrims coming to Jerusalem for the three pilgrimage Feasts: Unleavened Bread (Hag-HaMatzot), Pentecost (Shavu'ot), and Tabernacles (Sukkot)? It took 10,000 men ten years just to build the retaining walls. When they had finished, the platform was big enough to hold twenty-four football fields. Now that's big!

1. Read Deuteronomy 33:10, Numbers 1, 3:7-8, 4:1-49, 8:1-26 and 18:1-32. What was the role of the Levites in the tabernacle and temple?

Color the temple!

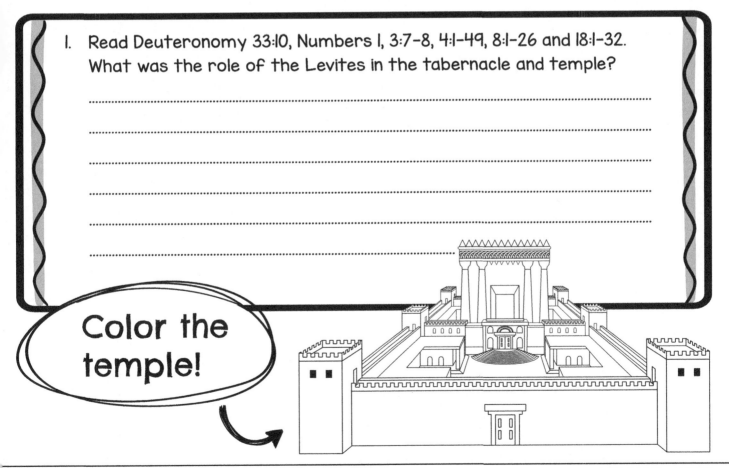

The Sabbath

Unscramble the words to find the answer. *Hint: Read Mark 2:27-28 (ESV).*

" hTe hatbabS aws edam

_____

for man, ton nma orf het

_____

Sbatabh. oS teh Son of aMn

_____

is odlr vnee of eht bbhatSa "

_____

Shabbat shalom

Honor the Sabbath

Read Luke 13:10-17 (ESV). Using the words below,
fill in the blanks to complete the Bible passage.

SYNAGOGUES	EIGHTEEN	SPIRIT	GLORIFIED
SABBATH	GLORIOUS	DONKEY	TEACHING
MANGER	HEALED	WOMAN	SIX

" He was .... in one of the .... on the Sabbath. And behold, there was a woman who had had a disabling .... for eighteen years. She was bent over and could not fully straighten herself. When Yeshua saw her, He called her over and said to her, ".............................., you are freed from your disability." He laid His hands on her, and immediately she was made straight, and she .... God. But the ruler of the synagogue, indignant because Yeshua had healed on the ...., said to the people, "There are .... days in which work ought to be done. Come on those days and be ...., and not on the Sabbath day." Yeshua answered him, "You hypocrites! Does not each of you on the Sabbath untie his ox or his .... from the .... and lead it away to water it? And ought not this woman, a daughter of Abraham whom Satan bound for .... years, be loosed from this bond on the Sabbath day?" As He said these things, all His adversaries were put to shame, and all the people rejoiced at all the .... things that were done by Him. "

Paul's first journey

The apostle Paul honored the Sabbath. While he traveled through Asia Minor, he taught people about the Messiah at many synagogue gatherings. To track Paul's first journey, read Acts 13-14 and find the locations he visited. Then, plot his expedition on the map.

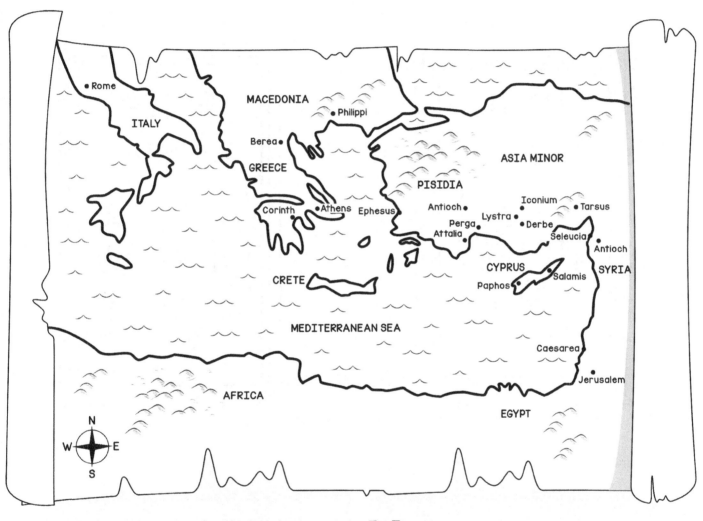

1. Antioch
2. Selucia
3. Salamis
4. Paphos
5. Perga
6. Pisidian Antioch
7. Iconium
8. Lystra
9. Derbe
10. Perga
11. Attalia

Keeping the Sabbath

Did Yeshua, the disciples and the apostle Paul keep the Sabbath?
Read the books of Matthew, Luke, John, and Acts 1, 13-18.
Find six Bible references where it shows they kept the Sabbath.

Let's discuss!

Open your Bibles and read the Bible verses below.
Discuss these questions in small groups with your friends, family, and classmates.

1 **Read Genesis 2:1-3.**
What is the Sabbath? Why did God give us the Sabbath?

2 **Read Exodus 20:8-11.**
Why do you think God included the Sabbath day in His ten commandments?

3 **Read Mark 2:27.**
What did Yeshua mean when He said, "The Sabbath was made for man, not man for the Sabbath"?

4 **Read Luke 4:14-30.**
What did Yeshua usually do on the Sabbath?

5 **Read Acts 13:1-20:7.**
Did Paul keep the Sabbath? How do you know?

6 How does your family honor the Sabbath?

✫ My Bible notes ✫

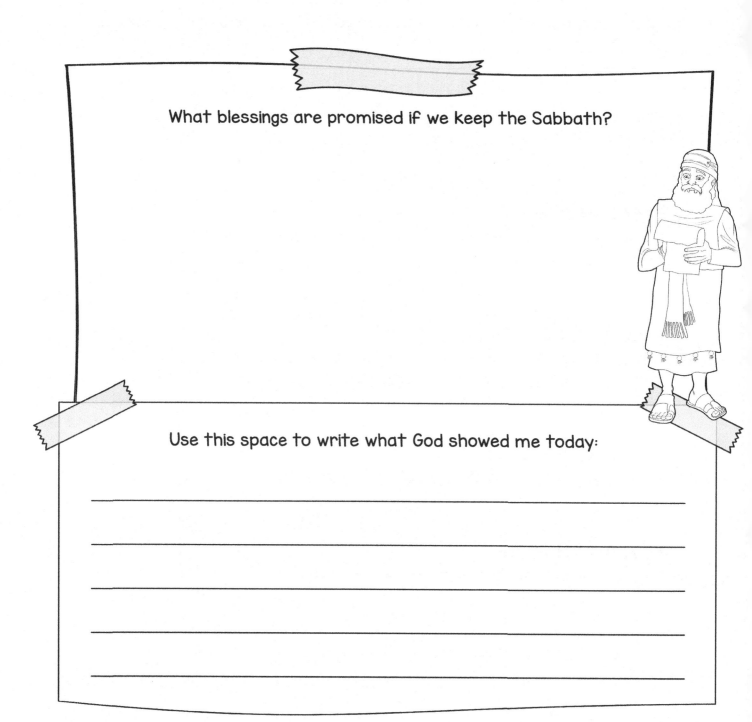

What blessings are promised if we keep the Sabbath?

Use this space to write what God showed me today:

_____

_____

_____

_____

_____

Creative writing

The ten commandments

1st commandment

Open your Bible and read Exodus 20:1-3.

Write a short paragraph to show how you honor this commandment.
Color the illustration at the bottom of the page.

....

....

....

....

....

....

....

2ⁿᵈ commandment

Open your Bible and read Exodus 20:4-6.

Write a short paragraph to show how you honor this commandment.
Color the illustration at the bottom of the page.

....

....

....

....

....

....

....

3rd commandment

Open your Bible and read Exodus 20:7.

Write a short paragraph to show how you honor this commandment.
Color the illustration at the bottom of the page.

....

....

....

....

....

....

....

4th commandment

Open your Bible and read Exodus 20:8-11.

Write a short paragraph to show how you honor this commandment.
Color the illustration at the bottom of the page.

....

....

....

....

....

....

....

5th commandment

Open your Bible and read Exodus 20:12.

Write a short paragraph to show how you honor this commandment.
Color the illustration at the bottom of the page.

....

....

....

....

....

....

6th commandment

Open your Bible and read Exodus 20:13.

Write a short paragraph to show how you honor this commandment.
Color the illustration at the bottom of the page.

....

....

....

....

....

....

....

7th commandment

Open your Bible and read Exodus 20:14.

Write a short paragraph about the importance of this commandment.
Color the illustration at the bottom of the page.

....

....

....

....

....

....

....

8th commandment

Open your Bible and read Exodus 20:15.

Write a short paragraph to show how you honor this commandment.
Color the illustration at the bottom of the page.

....

....

....

....

....

....

9th commandment

Open your Bible and read Exodus 20:16.

Write a short paragraph to show how you honor this commandment.
Color the illustration at the bottom of the page.

....

....

....

....

....

....

10th commandment

Open your Bible and read Exodus 20:17.

Write a short paragraph to show how you honor this commandment.
Color the illustration at the bottom of the page.

....

....

....

....

....

....

Crafts & Projects

ZEBULUN

5

EPHRAIM

6

MANASSEH

7

BENJAMIN

8

DAN

9

ASHER

10

GAD

11

NAPHTALI

12

The ten commandments

Instructions:

There are two sections to this craft:

1. Ten Commandments
2. Two Tablets

You will need:

1. Grey paint or crayons
2. Felt pens, crayons or coloring pencils
3. Extra-strength glue sticks or School glue

Instructions:

1. Cut out or print the ten commandments circle pages. Color the ten commandments circles.
2. Cut out or print the two tablet pages.
3. Cut out each commandment around the dotted edges.
4. Glue the tablets together by placing glue along the 'Glue Here' flap and seal together.
5. Glue the commandments in numerical order onto the two stone tablets – five on each side.

ta-da!

I AM YAHWEH YOUR GOD
- NO OTHER GODS

YOU SHALL MAKE
NO IDOLS

DO NOT MISUSE
GOD'S NAME

REMEMBER THE SABBATH

HONOR YOUR FATHER
AND MOTHER

YOU SHALL NOT
MURDER

YOU SHALL NOT
COMMIT ADULTERY

YOU SHALL NOT STEAL

YOU SHALL NOT BEAR FALSE
TESTIMONY AGAINST YOUR NEIGHBOR

YOU SHALL NOT COVET
YOUR NEIGHBOR'S THINGS

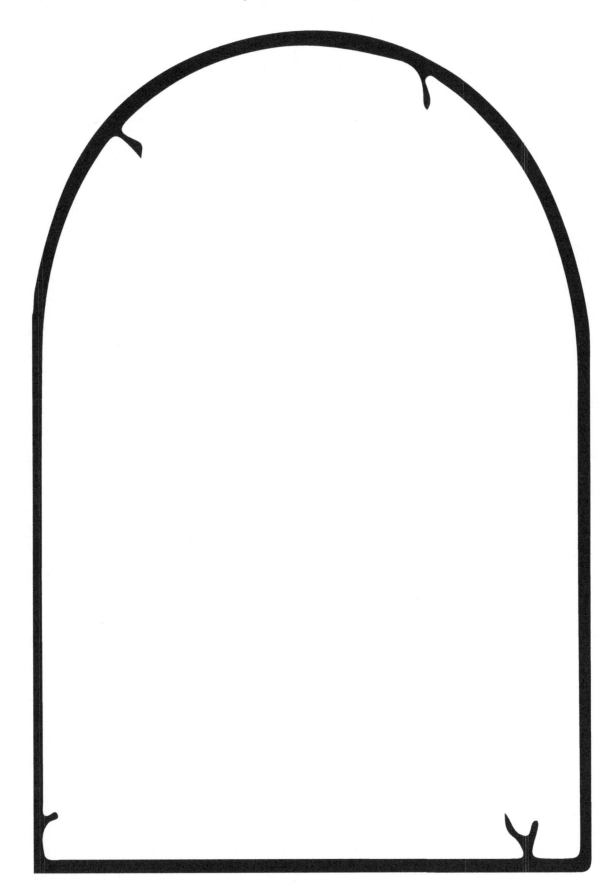

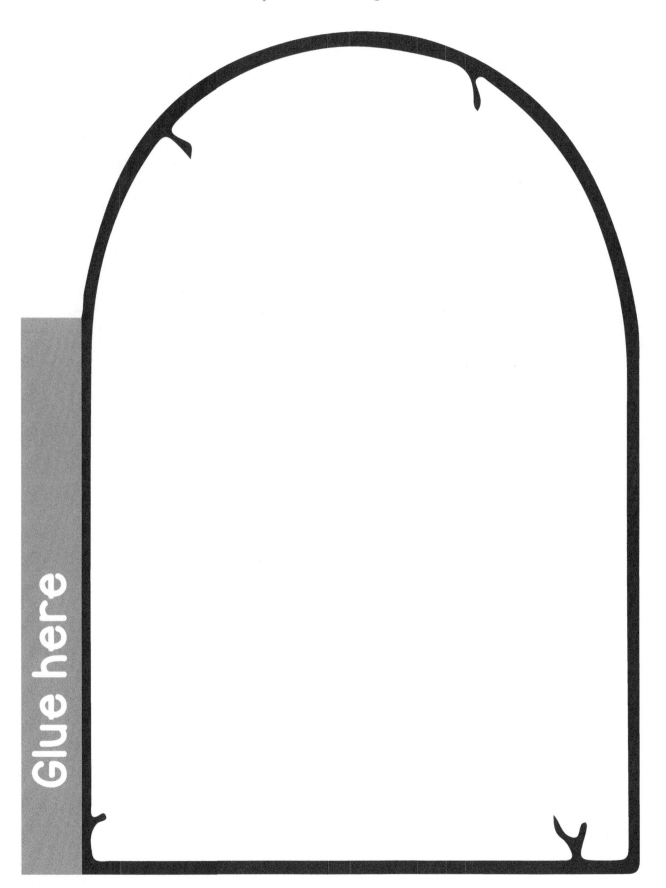

Glue here

"Remember the Sabbath day and keep it holy."

(Exodus 20:8)

Bible Pathway
— Adventures —

The Sabbath

Why did God give the
Israelites manna for
two days?

Bible verse lookup: Exodus 16:29

biblepathwayadventures.com

Card 1

The Sabbath

"Remember the Sabbath
day and keep it ____."

Bible verse lookup: Exodus 20:8

biblepathwayadventures.com

Card 2

The Sabbath

How did God tell the
Israelites to observe
the Sabbath?

Bible verse lookup: Deuteronomy 5:12-15

biblepathwayadventures.com

Card 3

The Sabbath

Why was the ruler of the
synagogue angry with
Yeshua in Luke 13?

Bible verse lookup: Luke 13:1-15

biblepathwayadventures.com

Card 4

Bible Pathway Adventures

Who said it?

Read Deuteronomy 5, Isaiah 56, Mark 2, and Hebrews 4. Color and cut out each Bible character. Match the Bible verse with the person who said it.

1. "So there remains a Sabbath rest for the people of God…" -Hebrews 4:9

2.  "The Sabbath was made for man, not man for the Sabbath." -Mark 2:27

3.  "But the seventh day is a Sabbath to the Lord your God." -Deuteronomy 5:14

4.  "Blessed is the man who does this, and the son of man who holds it fast, who keeps the Sabbath…" -Isaiah 56:2

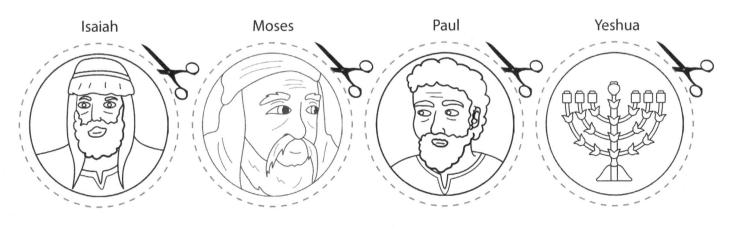

Isaiah   Moses   Paul   Yeshua

ANSWER KEY

What's the word? God rests

Thus the heavens and the earth were finished, and all the host of them. And on the seventh day God finished His work that He had done, and He rested on the seventh day from all His work that he had done. So God blessed the seventh day and made it holy, because on it God rested from all His work that He had done in creation. These are the generations of the heavens and the earth when they were created, in the day that God made the earth and the heavens. When no bush of the field was yet in the land and no small plant of the field had yet sprung up - for God had not caused it to rain on the land, and there was no man to work the ground, and a mist as going up from the land and was watering the whole face of the ground - then God formed the man of dust from the ground and breathed into his nostrils the breath of life, and the man became a living creature.

Bible word search puzzle: The Creation

Worksheet: Sabbath in the wilderness
Suggested answers:
1. God gave the Israelites quail, and rained manna from heaven for them to gather every day except for the Sabbath
2. God told the Israelites to rest on the Sabbath and not gather manna

Worksheet: Keeping the Sabbath
1. The new king over Egypt did not know Joseph
2. The Egyptians set taskmasters over the people of Israel to afflict them with heavy burdens, made them work as slaves, and made their lives bitter with hard service
3. The Israelites built store cities for Pharaoh, such as Pithom and Raamses

Worksheet: Discovering tzitzits
1. Tzitzits, also known as tassels, are a traditional Israelite garment used to fulfill one of God's commandments
2. Tzitzits are usually made of wool or linen, and are white and blue
3. The blue thread is known as a tekhelet and is a very important part of the tzitzits. It is a reminder of God's covenant with the Israelites

Worksheet: The ten commandments
1. I am Yahweh your God. You will have no other gods before Me.
2. You shall make no idols.
3. You shall not take the name of Elohim your God in vain.
4. Remember the Sabbath and keep it holy.
5. Honor your father and mother.
6. Do not murder.
7. Do not commit adultery.
8. Do not steal.
9. Do not give false testimony against your neighbor.
10. Do not desire other people's things.

Worksheet: Ark of the Covenant
Measurements for the mercy seat:
2 ½ cubits long
1 ½ cubits wide

Measurements for the ark:
2 ½ cubits long
1 ½ cubits wide
1 ½ cubits high

The ark and poles were made of pure gold.
The ark and poles were overlaid with pure gold.
The rings, mercy seat, and cherubim were made of pure gold.
There were two cherubim, four rings, and two poles.

Bible word scramble: Moses
observe, Sabbath, seventh, rest, Egypt, commanded, sojourner, mighty hand, servant, holy

Sabbath word match
1. C
2. E
3. G
4. A
5. B

6. D
7. H
8. F
9. J
10. I

Bible quiz: The Sabbath
1. The Sabbath
2. Almost the whole city
3. By the river
4. Three Sabbaths
5. Thessalonica
6. The Torah (law of Moses)
7. Went to the synagogue and discussed the Scriptures
8. For man
9. The Sabbath
10. Rest and do no servile work

Coloring worksheet: The Sabbath
1. Rest
2. The Sabbath
3. Six days

Bible puzzle: Did Yeshua keep the Sabbath?
"…as was His custom, He went to the synagogue on the Sabbath day, and He stood up to read."

Bible word search puzzle: The Sabbath

Worksheet: The Pharisees
1. Gamaliel, Paul (Saul), and Nicodemus
2. Yeshua entered a synagogue and healed a man's hand (Matthew 12:9-13)
3. Yeshua's twelve disciples were Simon Peter, Andrew, James (the son of Zebedee), John, Philip, Bartholomew, Thomas, Matthew, James (the son of Alphaeus), Thaddaeus, Simon the Zealot and Judas Iscariot

Worksheet: Temple in Jerusalem
The Levites' main roles in the temple included singing psalms during temple services, performing temple construction and maintenance, serving as guards, and performing other services. In the wilderness, they carried the tabernacle and its utensils, kept guard about the sanctuary, and performed various sacrifices and offerings. They were also teachers and judges, maintaining cities of refuge in biblical times.

Bible word scramble: The Sabbath
The Sabbath was made for man, not man for the Sabbath. So the Son of Man is lord even of the Sabbath.

Worksheet: Who said it?
1 = Paul, 2 = Yeshua, 3 = Moses, 4 = Isaiah

Worksheet: What's the Word?
He was teaching in one of the synagogues on the Sabbath. And behold, there was a woman who had had a disabling spirit for eighteen years. She was bent over and could not fully straighten herself. When Yeshua saw her, He called her over and said to her, "Woman, you are freed from your disability." He laid His hands on her, and immediately she was made straight, and she glorified God. But the ruler of the synagogue, indignant because Yeshua had healed on the Sabbath, said to the people, "There are six days in which work ought to be done. Come on those days and be healed, and not on the Sabbath day." Yeshua answered him, "You hypocrites! Does not each of you on the Sabbath untie his ox or his donkey from the manger and lead it away to water it? And ought not this woman, a daughter of Abraham whom Satan bound for eighteen years, be loosed from this bond on the Sabbath day?" As He said these things, all His adversaries were put to shame, and all the people rejoiced at all the glorious things that were done by Him.

Worksheet: Keeping the Sabbath
Matthew 12:1-14
Luke 13:10-17
John 5:1-8, 7:21-24
Acts 1:12
Acts 13:14, 27, 42, and 44
Acts 16:13
Acts 17:2
Acts 18:4

◦◇ DISCOVER MORE ACTIVITY BOOKS! ◇◦

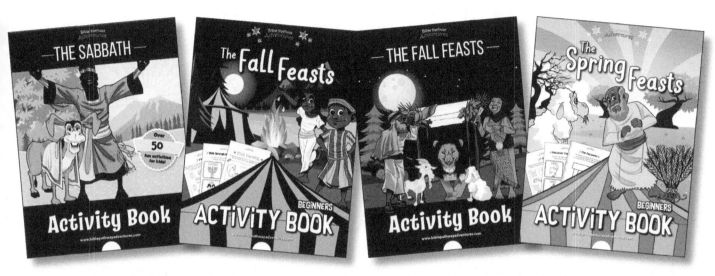

Available for purchase at shop.biblepathwayadventures.com

INSTANT DOWNLOAD!

The Sabbath	The Spring Feasts
The Fall Feasts (Beginners)	100 Bible Quizzes
The Fall Feasts	Fruit of the Spirit
The Spring Feasts (Beginners)	Learning Hebrew: The Alphabet

Made in the USA
Las Vegas, NV
29 November 2023

81820722R00052